Ludovic
KENNEDY

Euthanasia: The Good Death

Chatto & Windus
LONDON

Published in 1990 by
Chatto & Windus Ltd
20 Vauxhall Bridge Road
London SW1V 2SA

A CIP catalogue record for this book is available from the British Library

ISBN 0 7011 3639 1

Photoset in Linotron Ehrhardt by
Rowland Phototypesetting Ltd
Bury St Edmunds, Suffolk
Printed in Great Britain by
St Edmundsbury Press Ltd
Bury St Edmunds, Suffolk

Euthanasia

For help in the preparation of this pamphlet I am grateful to the Voluntary Euthanasia Society and its general secretary Mr John Oliver; the Dutch Voluntary Euthanasia Society and Mrs Jeane Tromp Meesters; Dr Pieter Admiraal, Dr Colin Brewer, Dr Herbert Cohen, Mrs Jean Davies, and Dr Andrew Reekie. I have also drawn on two books on the subject, *The Right to Die* by Derek Humphry and Ann Wickett (The Bodley Head, 1986) and *Voluntary Euthanasia*, edited by A. B. Downing and Barbara Smoker (Peter Owen, 1986).

L.K.

And in those days shall men seek death and shall not find it; and shall desire to die and death shall flee from them.

Revelations 9:6

WHEN MY mother was eighty she went to live in a private nursing home where I visited her regularly. She was not terminally ill in the sense of having cancer or some other fell disease, but her whole system had run down. Chronic arthritis and moments of giddiness kept her mostly in bed, and failing eyesight meant that she could no longer read or watch the television with any degree of enjoyment. In short, life had become a burden to her. When she was 83, and I asked her on one of my visits how she was, her answer surprised me: 'Oh, how I long to be gathered!' – the Scottish euphemism for death. On my subsequent visits she repeated this wish, adding that she had had a wonderful life, but the time had now come for it to end. But there was no means of ending it, and she survived for another year in increasing discomfort before I received a telephone call in the middle of the night that her wish had at last been granted.

Whether my mother would have been ready to

embrace voluntary euthanasia*, had it been available, I cannot say. But what I learned from her was something I had not realised before, that while today's world supports plenty of sprightly 90-year-olds, there are many other old people whose wish to die is no less strong than the wish of young people to live. Robert Louis Stevenson had the words to express it:

> 'It is not so much that death approaches as life withdraws and withers up from round about him. He has outlived his own usefulness and almost his own enjoyment; and if there is to be no recovery, if never again will he be young and strong and passionate . . . if in fact this be veritably nightfall, he will not wish for the continuance of a twilight that only strains and disappoints the eyes, but steadfastly await the perfect darkness.'

Yet every year there are an increasing number of increasingly old and sick people for whom the twilight continues unbearably and whose steadfastness in awaiting the perfect darkness often falls

* Throughout this pamphlet the term 'voluntary euthanasia' is used to denote medical assistance in terminating life *at the request of the patient and of no other.* Because deformed infants and those in a persistent vegetative state such as the advanced stages of Alzheimer's Disease are not in a position to volunteer anything, their cases have not been considered.

short of what they would wish; for the prolongation of living which has been brought about by advances in medical science has also meant the prolongation of dying. For millions of people whose span of life has been extended, its quality has been diminished. Some are in pain from cancer or have a wasting muscular disease: some are in acute discomfort from vomiting, diarrhoea, insomnia, bed sores, flatulence and general exhaustion, being fed by drips in the vein or tubes up the nose and into the stomach. The law at present does not allow doctors to grant them their pleas for merciful release. The compassion we show to sick animals by putting them out of their misery, we deny to our fellow human beings.

In the old days when most people died at home, the family doctor often felt no compunction in administering a lethal drug to help a dying patient on his or her way; but now that most people die in hospitals, doctors cannot do it without the knowledge of the nursing staff and thus, because it is a criminal offence, they endanger their professional careers. The most we can expect of doctors at present is the exercise of what is called passive euthanasia, that is the withholding of some life-sustaining drug or giving sufficient analgesics to alleviate pain yet which can also shorten life; but the effect of opiates such as morphine and heroin is by no means certain, and death can take a dismayingly long time. In the old days too pneumonia often came to give a terminally ill patient a quiet and comparatively speedy death; but today, when pneumonia sets in it is quelled with antibiotics which will keep the patient's heart beating for a few more miserable weeks or months.

Nor is it only the patient who suffers. In hospitals there are paid staff to look after the terminally ill. But at home the job often falls on the wife or daughter or husband, having to feed and wash and nurse, often for months on end, a loved one who no longer wishes to live and whose relentless deterioration they can only helplessly watch. 'Opponents of euthanasia,' says Professor Glanville Williams, 'are apt to take a cynical view of the desires of relatives . . . but it cannot be denied that a wife who has to nurse her husband through the last stages of some terrible disease may herself be so deeply affected by the experience that her health is ruined, either mentally or physically.'

There is another factor to be considered. Prolonged and painful dying, the gradual transformation of a much-loved parent or spouse or sibling from a familiar upright figure to that of a semi corpse can mean, when death finally comes, that they are not mourned. 'I had an excellent relationship with both my parents,' a woman wrote to me, 'but after watching the deterioration of their personalities and minds, caused by years of pain-killing and life saving drugs, watching their suffering and coping with their irrational behaviour, I was glad when they died.' Sorting through their letters, she remembered how close they had once been and felt guilty about not mourning them. 'Parents should go when they are remembered as their true selves. Parents *should* be mourned. That is the healthy, natural way.'

In recent years there have been distressing tales of how terminally ill people, unable to obtain deliverance from their doctors, have brought it about themselves. One was the writer and philosopher Arthur Koestler who only a couple of years earlier had written the preface to the Voluntary Euthanasia Society's *Guide to Self-Deliverance*. In this he said:

> 'Animals appear to give birth painlessly or with a minimum of discomfort. But owing to some quirk of evolution, the human foetus is too large for the birth canal, and its hazardous passage can entail protracted agony for the mother . . . Hence we need midwives to aid us to be born.
>
> A similar situation prevails at the exit gate. Animals in the wild, unless killed by a predator, seem to die peacefully and without fuss from old age . . . I cannot remember a single description to the contrary by a naturalist, ethologist or explorer. The conclusion is inescapable: we need midwives to aid us to be un-born . . . or at least the assurance that such aid is available. Euthanasia, like obstetrics, is the natural corrective to a biological handicap.'

But the midwife for whom Koestler had pleaded was not at hand for him when his own time came. On 3 March 1983, suffering from Parkinson's disease and advanced leukemia which he knew could only become worse, he and his wife took an overdose of barbiturates which he had hoarded over a period of time; and he left a note saying he wanted his friends to know he was leaving their company in a peaceful frame of mind.

Others have been less fortunate. The painter Rory McEwen, suffering from an inoperable brain tumour, threw himself under a train. Some have jumped from heights, shot or gassed themselves, and one young paraplegic, unable to contemplate further useless existence, set fire to himself fatally in the bungalow that had been specially equipped to house him.

These at least succeeded; but many more have failed. Here is what one correspondent recently wrote to me:

> 'I myself went through a harrowing experience with my beloved mother's final years. To see somebody you love suffering and daily getting worse is torture. She had very bad and very painful rheumatoid arthritis for several years before finally coming to live with us. The cortisone she was prescribed effectively destroyed her body, but death seemed as far off as ever.

At last she said, "Tonight I'm going to do it, I'm going to cut my arteries in my room." I never felt more helpless, more grief-stricken. I lay in bed in the next room, while she tried to kill herself with a pair of scissors. The horror of that night thirty years ago will be with me forever.

In the morning she was still alive, though she had lost a lot of blood. We sent for the doctor and, thank God – well, no, I don't thank God – we managed to get him to give her a quick release. But all that tragedy was so unnecessary: she could so easily have been spared that final agony.'

'This problem of the chronic sick and chronic pain-ridden,' he concluded, 'is the greatest social evil of the day and it's getting worse as the population ages. I am nearly seventy now, so meet a lot of old people, and their views on euthanasia are almost unanimous. No one wants to linger on, blind, crippled, in pain. All those in poor health want the option of deliverance, but lack the means, the knowhow, the courage, to do it themselves.'

A famous couplet by the poet Arthur Clough says, 'Thou shalt not kill but needst not strive / Officiously to keep alive.' But officiously keeping alive patients who wish to be dead is common hospital practice. Dr Christiaan Barnard, who pioneered transplant heart surgery, tells of what happened to a Mr Kahn. Aged 78, Mr Kahn had cancer of the prostate, obstruction of the bowel and severe emphysema. On admission to hospital he told the consultant quite calmly that he no longer wished to live, but the consultant told him that, in accordance with practice, his condition would be treated.

The man in the bed next to Mr Kahn was suffering from inoperable stomach cancer, and was totally unconscious with tubes connected to his abdomen, lungs and bladder. One day he had a heart attack which brought the resuscitation unit hurrying to his bedside. 'They did not know why his heart had arrested,' said Dr Barnard, 'and what quality of life he could be given if his heart was restarted. Their sole purpose was to restart the heart. They jumped on the old man, they massaged his heart from the outside, they shocked him and they ventilated his lungs.' To no avail: the man died. And Mr Kahn said to the consultant, 'Doctor, please promise that you will never let that happen to me, because I am a proud man and I do not fear death.' The consultant said nothing.

A few days later Mr Kahn developed problems with his lungs and they put a tube down his windpipe and connected him to a mechanical respirator to keep him alive; there was nothing he could do about it because he was now too weak to resist.

'That night,' continued Dr Barnard, 'when the nurse looked at Mr Kahn, she could see that the respirator was doing his breathing for him and that the monitor showed that his heart was beating. But in the morning Mr Kahn was dead. During the night he had managed to disconnect the respirator; and on the bed there was a note, written in a shaky hand. "Doctor, the real enemy is not death – it is inhumanity."' Dr Barnard is a fervent supporter of voluntary euthanasia. 'I have never practised it, but that is not something I am proud of; for, as a doctor, I have often seen the need for it.' He has however practised passive euthanasia, and on his own mother. 'After years of illness during which she often used to say, "Oh, why doesn't God take me?" she suffered a severe stroke. Her age was now 95 and she had suffered enough.'

> '. . . at that stage she could not swallow, and the hospital doctors had decided to pass a tube through her nose into her stomach to force-feed her. She also had pneumonia and they were going to give her antibiotics for that. Can you imagine greater madness? I said to my brother that the doctors must not be allowed to do these things to our mother. And she died two days later.'

In all the industrialised countries of the world stories like those can be multiplied almost indefinitely. Here is a letter from a 56-year-old retired Metropolitan Police Sergeant:

> 'I suffer from Buerger's Disease. I have had twelve general anaesthetic operations in University

> College Hospital . . . I have had just one amputation, half of my left foot. I had gangrene in all four limbs so the medical profession said it would be safer not to work. In winter my limbs are ice. In summer I perspire buckets.
>
> And now to plain talking. It is just a matter of time before another amputation is necessary due to the normal process of ageing. I will eventually become limbless. There is nothing the doctors can do. Therefore I shall just have to stay in a hospital bed suffering from the hellish pain of gangrene, waiting for another part of my body to be taken from me.'

The inability of this man and others like him to be granted the deliverance they seek has also resulted in recent years in an increasing number of mercy-killings. In a less understanding age those who carried out mercy-killings were often sentenced to imprisonment, but now a more compassionate attitude prevails. Here are one or two cases out of many submitted to the Royal Commission on Criminal Procedure by the Voluntary Euthanasia Society:

> A 26-year-old gardener was tried for murder at Nottingham Crown Court. He had put weed-killer in his mother's drink, as she was incurably ill and begged him to do so. The judge said, 'No one can

have anything but sympathy for you,' and gave him an absolute discharge.

Mrs Eva Lyons of Wanstead was charged with the murder of her mother-in-law who had several times tried to commit suicide, and finally begged her daughter-in-law to end her life. Mrs Lyons pleaded guilty to manslaughter with diminished responsibility and was given two years probation.

Mr Walter Saunders of Liverpool was due to appear in court charged with the murder of his wife. She had been suffering from a slowly worsening brain disorder and Mr Saunders was totally devoted to her. He ended her life with an overdose of drugs. On the day he was due to stand trial, Mr Saunders committed suicide.

In his book *Falling*, based on a true case, the writer Colin Thubron describes the plight of a young circus artist who falls from the high wire, fracturing her spine, and is totally paralysed in all her limbs. In hospital, because her respiratory muscles have gone, she is given a tracheotomy and connected to an artificial respirator, which will be permanent. Every two or three hours she is turned from side to side to prevent bed sores, and a catheter is inserted in her bladder: this too will be permanent. Within a few days she has contracted an infection. She knows that she will be dead within months and that what remains of her life is not worth living. So she says to her lover: 'You will help me to go, won't you?' And, in tears, he does. He gives her sleeping pills to swallow and with each gulp of water she says to him, 'Thank you, *Thank you.*' And when she is unconscious he disconnects the respirator that would keep her alive, to him a moral act if not a legal one.

There is also the story recounted in the book *Jean's Way* by Derek Humphry of how, when his wife Jean's cancer became unbearable, he promised he would give her a lethal draught which a doctor friend in London had specially prepared for him. The day arrived when she knew she must ask for it, and they sat together while she took the draught and presently died in his arms. Today Derek Humphry is the President of the World Federation of Right to Die Societies.

While we can be thankful that those who carry out mercy-killings rarely now have to endure imprisonment in addition to the other agonies they have been through, it seems dreadful, indeed shameful, that those they have helped to die were not permitted to call on professional help to enable them to do so.

In recent years the number of mercy-killings has, as you might expect, risen considerably, both here and in America, where of the 134 cases recorded since 1921 *no less than 70 per cent* took place between 1980 and 1985. In other words, the more that modern medicine has prolonged life, the more mercy-killings there have been. And parallel with these mercy-killings, parallel with the number of successful and attempted suicides, has been a growing recognition, all over the world, of the need for voluntary euthanasia.

In Britain a Mass Observation poll conducted in 1969 showed that 51 per cent of the population was in favour of it. Only seven years later an N.O.P. poll showed that this had risen to 69 per cent and by 1985 to 72 per cent. Recent polls in France and Canada have shown figures of more than 80 per cent, while in 1988 on the BBC television programme *Reportage*, targetted at those aged between 16 and 26, 7402 answered Yes and 692 No to the question: 'Should those who are terminally ill be allowed when to choose to die?' The British Voluntary Euthanasia Society, formed in 1935 with a handful of members, now has 10,000. In the United States membership of the Euthanasia Educational Council grew from 600 in 1969 to 300,000 in 1975. In several states bills to make euthanasia legal have been introduced but rejected. However, the concept of Living Wills (the early declaration by an adult that he or she does not wish to be kept artificially alive in certain circumstances) has been accepted by 36 state legislatures. In 1980 the World Right to Die Society was formed and now has 31 groups in 18 countries; while in America, England,

Scotland and Holland, manuals have been published on methods of committing suicide. In Holland the formation of a Voluntary Euthanasia Society in 1973 led a few years later to the practising of voluntary euthanasia by a few courageous medical pioneers. No less interesting have been the changing views of British doctors. An N.O.P. poll conducted in 1987 indicated that 35 per cent of doctors would be prepared to practise active euthanasia on request if it was made legal, and a further 10 per cent said they might possibly do so. Younger doctors were more in favour than older ones.

In this new climate, therefore, one has to ask, why does euthanasia at the request of the terminally ill still seem only a distant dream? Why do those in pain and discomfort, who want to die, have to be kept artificially alive? There are three answers. One is the British Medical Association, another is the Church, and the third is residual public opinion. But if the first two could be persuaded of euthanasia's merits, there is every reason to suppose that the third would be too.

SUICIDE, OR self-deliverance, has been practised as a release from the pains and exhaustion of old age by many societies in many ages. When an elderly Aymara Indian from Bolivia becomes terminally ill, his relatives and friends keep a vigil beside him. If death comes slowly, he may ask for assistance in dying, and then the family will withhold food and drink until he slips into unconsciousness. In some Eskimo cultures too, when an old person is ready for death he will ask his family to help him on his way. Pliny wrote of northern barbarian tribes whose old men jumped from overhanging rocks into the sea, 'having no pleasure to look forward to'. The Hottentots would give a feast to those who believed their time had come, and then abandon them in a hut in the wilderness to let nature take its course, while the Caritans regarded it as a noble task to stifle the dying 'to prevent their suffering'.

It was the Greeks who gave us the word *euthanasia* from *eu* (well) and *thanatos* (death), and it was one of the most famous of Greeks, Socrates, who, according to Pliny, preached that painful disease and suffering were impediments to continued living. He praised Asclepius, god of healing and medicine, for saying that he would not attempt to cure bodies which disease had penetrated through and through. 'He did not want to lengthen out good-for-nothing lives.' Socrates' own suicide was for moral rather than physical reasons, but the Stoics accepted suicide as a proper release from pain, grave illness or physical abnormalities. Cleanthes, a Stoic philosopher, was advised by his physician to starve himself to cure a boil. When the boil healed Cleanthes continued to starve. 'He had advanced too far on his journey towards death,' said his obituarist. 'He was ready to die.'

To the Romans suicide was also acceptable in certain circumstances: to avoid dishonour or disgrace at the hands of an enemy, or as a release from unendurable suffering. To them, as to the Greeks, dying well was as important as living well. 'It makes a great difference,' wrote the Stoic philosopher Seneca, 'whether a man is lengthening his life or his death. But if the body is useless for service, why should one not free the struggling soul?' And anticipating the Living Wills of the late twentieth century, he added, 'Perhaps one ought to do this a little before the debt is due, lest when it falls due, he may be unable to perform the act.'

Then came Christianity and in time an end to the idea of suicide as a noble death. For Christians suicide was a mortal sin because of their belief that one's life belonged to 'God'. Christians who killed themselves were denied Christian burial: a suicide's goods were confiscated and his body, impaled with a stake, was buried by the highway. By the fifth century St Augustine was calling suicide 'detestable and damnable wickedness': suffering was ordained by 'God' and must be recognised as His will. In 693 the Council of Toledo declared that failed suicides would be excommunicated; and the height of intolerance towards them was reached in the thirteenth century by St Thomas Aquinas. Suicide, he said, violated the Sixth Commandment, left no time for repentance, was contrary to nature and a violation of 'God's' purpose. Twelve centuries after the death of Christ (who had never pronounced on the matter) it had become the most mortal of sins.

With the Renaissance and a greater emphasis on individualism, some enlightenment set in. In the ideal society which Sir Thomas More envisaged in *Utopia*, he suggested that priests and officials who visited those afflicted with constant, excruciating pain should urge them to escape to a better world. 'If the patient finds these arguments convincing, he either starves himself to death or is given a soporific and put painlessly out of his misery. *But this is strictly voluntary*' (my italics). Montaigne too thought that suicide could be justified. 'Death is a most assured haven, never to be feared and often to be sought.' As man was going to die anyway, what difference

After declaring suicide to be as wrong as murder, the Pope went on:

> 'It is necessary to state firmly once more that nothing and no one can in any way permit the killing of an innocent human being, whether . . . an old person or one suffering from an incurable disease or a person who is dying. Furthermore no one is permitted to ask for this act of killing, either for himself or herself . . . nor can he or she consent to it, either explicitly or implicitly. For it is a question of the violation of the divine law, a crime against life and an attack on humanity.'

This cruel pronouncement was then compounded by a statement of sheer ignorance:

> 'The pleas of gravely ill people who sometimes ask for death are not to be understood as implying a true desire for euthanasia; in fact it is almost always a case of an anguished plea for help and love.'

One would like to hear the Pope repeat that to someone suffering from terminal cancer of the bowel, doubly incontinent and being fed through a tube in the nose. But the Pope is incorrigible; he even has a word of cheer about suffering:

> 'According to Christian teaching, suffering, especially suffering during the last moments of life,

has a special place in God's saving plan; it is in fact a sharing in Christ's Passion and a union with the redeeming sacrifice which He offered in obedience to the Father's will.'

I imagine that to most people today those views will be regarded as tosh and, what is more, pernicious tosh; for there will always be those wanting others to do their thinking for them. Indeed, in a 1987 N.O.P. poll of general practitioners only 22 per cent of Roman Catholic doctors agreed with the concept of voluntary euthanasia while 66 per cent disagreed; a figure bound to have been reflected in the 54 per cent of all GPs who would be unwilling to practise voluntary euthanasia even if it were made legal.

Yet religious opponents to euthanasia and suicide must be an ever-diminishing band for, as Mary Rose Barrington says, 'people are ever more detached from dogmas and revelationary teachings about right and wrong'; ever more detached too from the concept of immortal life. In this connection it is interesting to note that a religious breakdown of the 1985 N.O.P. poll showed that 89 per cent of atheists were in favour of euthanasia, 84 per cent of Jews, 75 per cent of Church of England, while of Roman Catholics, who might have been expected not to want to delay their passage to Elysium, only 54 per cent . . . a majority nevertheless.

Indeed, after the Roman Catholic Church, the greatest opposition to euthanasia comes from the medical profession and, in particular, the British Medical Association. In 1988 the BMA published a booklet setting out the reasons for their opposition and, choosing my words carefully, I have to say that it is one of the most prejudiced, irresponsible and cowardly documents to emanate from a professional body that I have ever read. But when you remember what a deeply reactionary institution the BMA has always been, for years setting its face against the introduction first of contraception and then of abortion, it is perhaps not all that surprising.

The reason the booklet is all I have said is that the profession refuses to recognise the consequence of its own technological progress, and while this has resulted in prolonged and satisfactory living for some, it has also led to prolonged and miserable dying for others. Grudgingly admitting that patients now have a right to have a voice in what is to be done to them, the authors query whether this right is absolute; and from there it is an easy step to assume the old paternalism, pretend that it is the doctors who are being asked to decide when euthanasia should be administered, when every pro-euthanasia group in the world, and in Holland where it is practised, insist that it is the patient and only the patient who shall be entitled to make that decision.

The whole booklet is shot through with this false assumption, which naturally its authors have little trouble in disposing of; and to strengthen their bogus case they eschew the phrase 'aid in dying' used by Dutch doctors and pro-euthanasia groups in favour of 'putting away', 'dispatching', 'killing'. (As Jean Davies has pointed out, words like 'killing' and 'rape' posit acts which do not have the receiver's consent, whereas 'aid in dying' and 'making love' do.) They quote with apparent pride the irrelevant and distasteful words of a Florida physician: 'We shall start by putting patients away because they are in intolerable pain and haven't long to live anyway, and we shall end by putting them away because it's Friday night and we want to get away for the weekend.' They talk about the circumstances 'in which doctors can intervene to end someone's life' when intervention is the last thing they should be allowed to do; and they have this to say on the subject of the elderly: 'It is in this group of patients who might be killed allegedly in their best interests that there is cause to fear a slide into practices which all would find abhorrent.' Approving of medical practice which allows dying patients to die, the booklet says: 'What is not acceptable is that doctors should take the step of dispatching such patients for the convenience and comfort of others.' Quite. But no one is asking them to.

The booklet again refuses to face the problems

by saying that it is now possible to give opiates to ease pain 'for many weeks or months without killing the patient', but does not question what the patient's frame of mind might be during the weeks and months he or she is kept going, and indeed whether they any longer want to be kept going. Similarly with those suffering from spinal trauma, multiple sclerosis and other crippling diseases. 'It is a far more demanding and challenging task to attempt to discover value in the terrible situation that exists,' says the booklet, 'than to kill the patient.' One is entitled to ask, value for whom, the patient or the doctor? If the patient can find value in his present state, well and good. But if he cannot and wishes to die, why refuse him help in doing so?

Then, again avoiding the issue, the report suggests that the reason that *many* (my italics) dying patients ask to have their lives terminated is 'as tests to see if they are still valued as individuals'. It goes on: 'If these individuals are right in the supposition that their lives have little value, agreeing to kill them will confirm that belief.' What the BMA does not seem to understand is that for these people life *has lost* its value, and in their readiness to admit it, they are showing a courage in facing reality which the BMA and its supporters conspicuously lack.

The report puts forward two further arguments to defend its opposition to euthanasia: firstly that life is 'God-given', secondly that it is 'sacred'. For the first the report relies on its great anti-euthanasia ally, the Church, and quotes the Archbishop of York as seeing death as a surrender into the hands of 'God' – though it is hard to think that 'God' would mind if a believer decided to surrender himself sooner rather than later. And because life is 'God-given', it is claimed, it is not for doctors to play at being 'God' by shortening it: nature must be allowed to take its course. But doctors play at 'God' and interfere with nature all the time: when they remove a tumour or transplant a kidney or perform a heart bypass, they are interfering with nature; and if they do this to lengthen life for good purpose, why not to abbreviate it for good purpose too?

The argument about life being sacred is nonsense. It is always held up as a cardinal belief of any civilised society, but throughout history it has been practised more in the breach than the observance. Societies which engage in wars do not respect the sanctity of life. Societies which execute their murderers and require of their doctors that they examine the condemned man to see if he is fit to die and later to attend his execution do not respect the sanctity of life. And societies which permit their doctors to perform abortions do not respect it either; for while a foetus may not be an independent living being, nobody can deny that, like a bud or a chrysalis it is a form of life; and it is hard to understand how doctors who can routinely bring to an end life which has barely begun can yet baulk at being asked to do so to lives which are all but over.

Passive euthanasia, that is alleviating pain or discomfort with the administering or withdrawal of drugs, the effect of which will be to shorten life, is as far as most doctors are prepared to go. In this they have the blessing of the Archbishop of York, who sees a difference between 'administering a treatment however potentially lethal, and administering a drug which has no beneficial effects apart from killing the patient'. Yet the report does have the courage to admit that it has been put to the BMA that this is mere playing with words, that ethically there is no difference between the two. This is the view of many doctors, lawyers and moralists, among them Dr Christiaan Barnard and Dr Joseph Fletcher, a Professor of Social Ethics and Moral Theology in Cambridge, Massachusetts and Visiting Professor of Medical Ethics at the University of Virginia. 'It is naïve and superficial,' writes Dr Fletcher, 'to suppose that because doctors don't do anything *positively* to hasten a patient's death, they have thereby avoided complicity in his death. *Not doing anything is doing something.* It is a decision to act every bit as much as a decision for any other deed.' Whatever the intent of our actions, the known consequence is all; so that the action of a doctor who gives a massive dose of morphine to release, a final act of compassion and love. It is compassion that is the mainspring of all mercy killings; but this is not a sentiment that features in the BMA report.

Let it not be thought though that the views expressed by the BMA report are shared by every doctor in the country. There are many, young and old, who disagree. Dr Stephen Henderson-Smith from Huddersfield recently recalled being asked by a patient suffering from bronchitis and emphysema so that every breath was an agony, how many sleeping pills he should take 'to switch it all off'. The doctor told him, and a week later heard that the patient had died. 'I didn't feel at all guilty about it,' he said. 'I felt I'd done for him what I would like someone to do for me.' He added: 'People should plan for dying as they plan for moving house.' Dr Jonathan Miller, the film and theatrical producer, agrees. 'Everyone ought to be able to choose when and how they die and get medical help to do so.' He admits that some doctors do help patients on their way, 'but while voluntary euthanasia is illegal, *they should not be put in this position*.' If it were legal, he says, and someone asked him to help them to die, he would. And the psychiatrist Dr David Clark recalls the time when he was a medical student and his chief gave a young man in agony from advanced tuberculosis of the stomach a lethal injection to put him out of his misery. 'Ever since that time,' he writes, 'I have been a convinced believer in the propriety of euthanasia and have supported the cause of voluntary euthanasia. I should certainly wish it for myself if it were ever necessary.'

One person who would never wish it for herself or indeed for others is the formidable founder of the hospice movement in Britain, Dame Cicely Saunders. As a nurse Dame Cicely was appalled at how little time and attention nurses in hospitals were able to give to those dying of cancer in pain and loneliness. So, having qualified as a doctor, she set about raising funds to establish a number of hospices, small self-contained hospital units holding no more than perhaps twenty beds. Here terminal cancer patients are given individual nursing care, including enough pain killers to dull all but a fraction of the worst pain, so that they may end their days in as tranquil a state of mind as possible. Some years ago, I made several visits to one of these hospices where a friend of mine was dying, and was much impressed by its atmosphere of peace and calm. Dame Cicely and her staff have been pioneers in techniques of pain control, about which they give advice and lectures in hospitals and medical centres all over the country; and their nurses go out to care for patients in their homes.

But there are two snags to the hospice movement. The first is that they are not and can never be an alternative to euthanasia, for there are not enough of them. Some 150,000 people die of cancer in Britain every year, and the total number of beds in all the hospices combined is less than 2000. The second objection is that it is well known that, being founded on Christian principles (Dame Cicely is herself a committed Christian) they will not entertain euthanasia at any price, even as a last option. 'Very few people ask for it,' says Dame Cicely, a remark which led Dr Herbert Cohen in Holland to say to me, 'Very few people think of asking for a steak in a vegetarian restaurant.' But the house rules are inflexible.

Yet every now and again the inmates do ask for it, as was admitted when an annual report of the St Christopher Hospice, of which Dame Cicely is a director, discussed the case of a Mrs N, a 65-year-old former nurse. Mrs N had a secondary tumour in the armpit which was so painful that her dosage of morphine had to be increased from 120mg every four hours to 150mg and then to 180mg, with an additional injection of Palfium (another morphine-type drug) before the tumour was dressed. When the tumour extended down her arm, but with her mind still acute, she made the first of several pleas for release. 'You wouldn't let this happen to a puppy-dog, would you?' she said, and the report admits that this was a difficult question to answer.

As the days passed, Mrs N's medication was increased until she was getting doses of 120mg of heroin (much stronger than morphine) with further doses of Palfium in between. Her last moments came, as she hoped they would, as the result of a haemorrhage, when she was heard to call out drowsily, 'Help, help!' Whereupon someone said to her, 'God loves you, Mrs N,' to which Mrs N, who was a known freethinker, replied, 'No, he doesn't.' The homily was repeated, and Mrs N this time replied, no doubt to bring the conversation to an end, 'Well, maybe he does.'

This somewhat vacuous exchange deeply impressed the writer of the report, who concluded that Mrs N's last words 'would always stick in our minds'.

They also stuck in the mind of the psychiatrist Dr Colin Brewer, who felt that to offer dubious theological advice to a non-believer in her dying moments was at best unnecessary and at worst offensive. He understood that Mrs N's requests for release could not be met because of the house rules, but it seemed to him that in this case at least there was a clear need for it. Nor could he believe that such a case was unique or even unusual. For all the good work that it has done Dr Brewer considers the hospice movement's denial of choice to be totalitarian; while Dr Henderson-Smith finds 'a sense of self-righteousness coupled with an arrogance which is patronising in its implications'. When I saw Dame Cicely on a television programme utter the scaremongering parrot-cry, 'Of course if ever euthanasia was legalised, it wouldn't be voluntary for long,' I realised that this was not a matter to which she had given any serious consideration or study. What she was concerned with, it seemed to me, was the threat that euthanasia posed to the ideals that had governed her life's work; that it was a rival that had, so to speak, to be smothered at birth.

THE DUTCH are an intriguing people; they are the legatees of Calvinism, yet they have one of the most progressive penal systems in Europe; they are both exhibitors and exporters of hard-core pornography; and they are the first people in the world to accept, though not yet to legalise, active euthanasia. 'We are both stubborn and tolerant,' one of them said to me, 'and we can't see why others should prevent us having what we want.'

Like their fellow countrymen the doctors of the Netherlands have a reputation for fierce independence, a quality which gained them much praise during the war when, despite threats and the withdrawal of their licences, they refused to play any part in the Nazi programme of sterilisation of and medical experiments on Jews, gypsies and mental defectives; and it was this assertion of independence combined with great moral courage that resulted in a case that was to herald the advent of active euthanasia.

In October 1971 the mother of Dr Gertrude Postma, a general practitioner, was a patient in a nursing home where she had been severely ill for some time. She had had a cerebral haemorrhage, was partly paralysed, had difficulty in speaking and was deaf. She had tried and failed to commit suicide, and on several occasions had begged her daughter to bring her misery to an end. For some time Dr Postma felt unable to comply, but one day when she went to the nursing home she found her mother propped up in a chair, tied to its arms to prevent her falling over. It was the last straw. 'When I saw my mother hanging in that chair, a human wreck,' she said, 'I couldn't stand it any more,' and the next day she met her mother's wishes by injecting into her veins a lethal dose of morphine.

In due course Dr Postma was indicted for mercy-killing, which then carried a maximum penalty of twelve years imprisonment. Asked at her trial if her mother's suffering was unbearable, she replied candidly, 'No, it was not unbearable, though it was serious. But her mental suffering *was* unbearable.' Asked if she had any regrets, she said, 'On the contrary, I am convinced I should have done it much earlier.' Instead of the prison term she might have expected, she was given a week's suspended sentence and a year's probation. Not only did this win the approval of the general public, but a number of fellow doctors wrote to the Minister of Justice to say they had done the same thing themselves.

This landmark case opened the way for the formation, in Dr Postma's village, of a Society for Voluntary Euthanasia, from which tiny beginnings it soon expanded to become what it still is today, the largest voluntary euthanasia society in Europe with a membership of 35,000. Since its inception it has had two objects. Firstly to act as an information centre for those mostly elderly and often lonely people who, while not actively seeking euthanasia, want to know more about it; and secondly to give guidance to those seeking euthanasia because of an incurable disease or infirmity. All members are advised to make Living Wills to indicate to their doctors that, should they ever deteriorate into a vegetative state where they can no longer make rational decisions, they do not wish to be kept artificially alive.

In 1976 the Society began recruiting volunteers, mostly over 50 years of age, to act as counsellors to those expressing a wish to die. These counsellors (there are now some 40 of them) visit the members concerned, assess the extent of their suffering and whether they think everything possible is still being done for them, what sort of family support they have, whether their wish for death is strongly held and entirely their own, and their relationship with their general practitioner. Often the volunteers find that those who want death are reluctant to broach the subject with their doctors, either because they have grown fond of them over many years, or because they fear the doctor may be anti-euthanasia. In such cases the Society, with the member's permission, tells the doctor what has been said to them, so that he may then approach the patient himself. This has proved very beneficial, as many doctors are themselves reluctant to discuss with their patients the question of their deaths. Most applicants are cancer sufferers, some suffer from multiple sclerosis, rheumatism or emphysema, others simply feel they have lived long enough. If the applicant's own doctor is unwilling to help him or her in bringing on death, the Society will endeavour to make contact with a doctor who is willing, provided there is sufficient time for the doctor to get to know and care for the patient.

In 1980, with opinion polls showing that more than 70 per cent of the Dutch people (of whom 40 per cent are Roman Catholic) were in favour of voluntary euthanasia, the Society published a booklet entitled *Justifiable Euthanasia* advising the country's 19,000 doctors and 2,000 pharmacists of the most suitable drugs for the administration of euthanasia. Another 10,000 copies were sold to the public. Derek Humphry's book, *Let Me Die Before I Wake*, containing similar information, was published in the United States at about the same time.

In 1981, in response to the growing demand and practice of euthanasia by the medical profession, the Rotterdam criminal court set out certain guidelines for euthanasia which, if followed, would be unlikely to render the doctor concerned liable for prosecution:

1. There must be physical or mental suffering which the patient finds unbearable.
2. The wish to die must be sustained.
3. The decision to die must be the voluntary act, given in writing, of the patient.
4. The patient must have a clear understanding of his condition and of any other possibilities in the way of treatment open to him.
5. No other solution is acceptable to the patient.
6. The time and manner of death must not cause avoidable misery to the patient's family, who should be kept informed of the situation at all stages.
7. The decision to give aid in dying must not be that of one doctor alone. Another doctor, who has no professional or social relationship with the first, must be consulted and give his approval.
8. Only a fully qualified doctor will prescribe the correct drugs and administer them.
9. The decision to give aid in dying and the actual administering of it must be done with the utmost care.
10. The patient need not be terminally ill (i.e. the decision could be that of a paraplegic).

Soon after the issuing of these rules, another case arose which was to further advance the cause of euthanasia. A 94-year-old woman, a patient in a nursing home, in poor health for some time and who had repeatedly asked her doctor for euthanasia, fractured her hip in a fall. As a result she became totally bedridden, had to be catheterised and was wholly dependent on the nursing staff for washing and all bodily functions: in time her sight and hearing declined, she was unable to drink or take solid food and had difficulty in speaking; and once again, but even more urgently, she begged her doctor for release. As she had signed a Living Will several years previously, the doctor consulted with another doctor and after a conference with him, the patient and the patient's son, he agreed to act. 'This doctor,' she told her son, 'deserves great respect.' After she had said goodbye to her son and his wife, the two doctors entered her room and asked if her wish was still the same, to which she replied, 'Straightaway, doctor, if it is possible. Please, not another night.' Her doctor then gave her three injections, the first of barbiturates to send her to sleep, another of barbiturates to induce a coma, and the last of curare to bring about respiratory arrest.

Having written 'Unnatural death' on the death certificate, the doctor was brought to trial in the district of Alkmaar and acquitted. The public prosecutor however appealed against the verdict, submitting that what the doctor had done was a violation of Section 293 of the Dutch Criminal Code ('Any person who takes the life of another at his or her explicit request shall be sentenced to a term of imprisonment not exceeding twelve years'), and the Court of Appeal agreed. The case then went to the Netherlands Supreme Court and their opinion was that the doctor was justified in what he did, in that he believed and his patient believed that there was no satisfactory alternative. In referring the case back to the Court of Appeal for reconsideration, the Supreme Court broke new ground in declaring that the primary judgement in cases of medical euthanasia should be *the responsibility of the medical profession*, and so should not be considered as a violation of the Criminal Code. 'Like the surgeon who has to harm the patient with a scalpel but is not prosecuted for battery,' said Eugene Sutorious, the doctor's attorney, 'so will voluntary euthanasia as a final part of medical practice remain unpunished under the very strict conditions to be set up by the medical profession itself.'

Since then voluntary euthanasia in Holland has become commonplace, although there are many doctors who refuse to practise it while it is still illegal. It is believed that between 2,000 and 5,000 patients are helped to die each year, but as many doctors, to spare grieving relatives from intrusive and distressing police questioning and the removal of the corpse for post-mortem, continue to write

'Natural causes' on the death certificate, no accurate figure can be given. Although in such cases there is no room for abuse in that the doctor has followed the rules laid down by the Rotterdam Court (obtained the patient's written declaration, consulted another doctor and the next of kin, etc.) the Royal Dutch Medical Association has instructed its members to comply with the legal requirements ('not filling in forms truthfully is unbefitting a physician'), while making recommendations that in future questioning is less intrusive. This has already borne fruit with the result that many more cases of euthanasia are now being reported.

Several years ago there was a concerted movement in Holland to make euthanasia legal by a simple amendment to exempt doctors from Sections 293 and 294 (penalty for assisted suicide) of the Criminal Code. But before it could be debated in Parliament, a new government was elected consisting of a coalition of Christian Democrats, who are anti-euthanasia, and Socialists who are for it. No euthanasia Bill therefore will be passed during the lifetime of the present Parliament, although the government has set up a commission to study the whole question. It is interesting to note that many doctors who practise euthanasia do not want to see it legalised, because they think it almost impossible to interpret ('How do you define degrees of suffering?' one said to me), and because they fear it could lead to abuse. They endorse the view of the Supreme Court in the case of the 94-year-old woman that it is to the medical profession *and not* to the police and the courts that they should report cases of euthanasia; but that Sections 293 and 294 should remain on the statute book as ultimate safeguards against wrongdoing.

If one had to name one Dutch doctor who has been in the forefront of the euthanasia movement in Holland, it is Pieter Admiraal, senior anaesthetist at Reinier de Graaf Hospital in Delft and the author of the booklet *Justifiable Euthanasia* already referred to. Now aged 60, he has performed many acts of euthanasia which he defines as 'a deliberate life-shortening act in respect of an incurable patient, done so that a quick peaceful death ensues', and which he himself sees as 'a dignified last act of medical care for a patient in his terminal phase'. He has become famous because, from the first case he handled, he was entirely open about what he did. And he expresses his philosophy in simple terms: 'Every patient has the right to ask for euthanasia. Every doctor has the right to perform euthanasia. Every doctor has the right to refuse it. But it is the patient who must make the decision.'

Dr Admiraal greatly deplores the fact that so many doctors are reluctant to tell the patient the truth about their illness, especially when it is likely to be terminal. 'It is the doctor's responsibility to tell the patient the truth, for it is he in whom the patient has put his trust.' He thinks it quite wrong that the family be told that the patient is terminally ill but that the patient himself be kept in the dark, imagining the worst. In his own hospital about 150 patients die of cancer each year, some 10 per cent of them as a result of euthanasia. After diagnosis the patient is fully informed of the nature of his or her illness, the treatment available, and its likely course, including the possibility of its being terminal. 'The attitude of a patient who is prepared to die is totally different from that of one who nurtures a false hope of survival.'

Few patients ask their doctor for euthanasia as such, but might say to him or, more likely, to one of the nurses, 'I don't want to go on like this.' Then the doctor will talk to the patient, find out whether the desire to be given release is well-founded or simply whether he or she feels that not enough is being done for them. Either way the nurses have an important part to play, described by one, Marjon Boschman, as, 'to take time to sit quietly at the patient's side, to create an atmosphere of calm and sympathy where the patient feels he can say anything he wishes, to protect the patient against unnecessary medical intervention, and to give maximum nursing support as long as possible', a similar role to that employed in hospices. If the desire for death is well-founded and sustained, Dr Admiraal will discuss the situation openly with the other doctors, the patient, the nursing staff, the pastor and the patient's family. 'Occasionally a patient will say without warning, "I want to die as soon as possible," and then I have to ask them to hold out for a little while, so that their family can get accustomed to the idea and find it more acceptable.' Sometimes, because patients are as reluctant as doctors to talk about their deaths, he will introduce the option of euthanasia himself. 'It can be of great comfort and of great value for many a patient to know that the option is open to him.'

Dr Admiraal will not agree to perform euthanasia on cancer patients on grounds of pain alone, for pain today can mostly be relieved by nerve blocks or drugs. It has to be pain plus sufferings such as psychic disturbances, breathlessness, vomiting, gangrene, oedema and the loss of the will to live. In their terminal stages cancer patients are put in a room by themselves. 'The consequent isolation intensifies the loneliness of a cancer patient, especially at night. Nights are long, silent and dark. It is normal for a patient being immobile not to sleep very well. An hour without sleep seems endless. Often the patient is nervous and depressed, sorrowful about the family he is to leave behind.' For many of these terminal patients the thought of euthanasia comes as a blessed relief.

When the patient's family come to take final leave of him or her before euthanasia is given, the patient, if it is at all feasible, will ask for a shave or hairwash and fresh pyjamas or nightgown so that the family's final memory will be a happy one. Inevitably for the family this will be an occasion of much grief, yet also therapeutic. When the family have gone, the nursing team will come in, often accompanied by the hospital chaplain, whom Dr Admiraal feels contributes to what he calls 'the choreography of the proceedings' and whose comforting presence even an unbelieving patient is sometimes glad to have.

All acceptable methods of euthanasia in Holland are contained in a manual published by the Dutch Royal Society of Pharmacists and have been approved by the Dutch Royal Society of Medicine. Among general practitioners the most common practice is to hand the patient a draught containing a mixture of barbiturate and a drug called Orphenadrine, which results in rapid loss of consciousness followed by death within an hour. 'For the patient and his family,' says Dr Admiraal, 'this method, whereby the patient takes the drug on his own, is of great psychological importance.' In his own hospital however, where some patients have difficulty in swallowing, and where the progress of all terminal patients has been regularly monitored for a long time, he prefers either an infusion of barbiturate fed by drip into the vein, or an injection into the vein of barbiturate followed by an opiate. Drugs such as morphine, curare and depronal are used, but Dr Admiraal stresses that the choice and dosage of drug very much depends on the patient's medical history and whether he has developed a tolerance towards any of them. There is no place in his scheme of things for 'passive' euthanasia, for in only one or two instances (e.g. artificial ventilation) will death occur quickly. 'In all the others it will be long; many days, perhaps even weeks. During that time the patient will suffer in different ways. Would anybody dare to assert that this amounts to the peaceful death as desired by the patient and his family?'

While in Holland I also spoke to another well-known doctor who practises euthanasia, Herbert Cohen, a general practitioner. Unlike Dr Admiraal, the patients he attends are either in nursing homes or at home. 70 per cent of his patients who are terminally ill have cancer, 15 per cent motor neurone disease or multiple sclerosis and the remainder rheumatism, diabetes, kidney disease, etc. Sometimes he is called in by patients of other doctors who do not practise euthanasia, but stresses he must have time to get to know them. He refuses to write a cause of death on the death certificate, but like Dr Admiraal, calls in the police and tells them what he has done. He strongly believes that in future all euthanasia cases should be reported only to the coroner, and not to the police, so that if the coroner had grounds for concern he could pass the case to the Public Prosecutor. Like Dr Admiraal, Dr Cohen is in no hurry to see euthanasia legalised, believing that the difficulties of interpretation in any Act could raise more problems than they would solve.

Drs Admiraal, Cohen and other doctors who practise euthanasia, do not find it easy, it being so opposed to all they have been taught. Dr Admiraal told me, 'To help to end the life of a patient I know well, even though he has asked for it, can be deeply upsetting.' And Dr Cohen says, 'I never do more than one a month. Emotionally I find it very burdensome.' But both doctors agree that their own discomfort is a small price to pay for alleviating the misery of those patients to whom they have pledged release.

Both doctors also believe that euthanasia's time has come; that opinion polls show that it is now a world movement whose impetus cannot and should not be stopped. Dr Admiraal says, 'By the year 2030 more than half the population of Europe will be over 60, so that demands for it are bound to increase.' Dr Cohen agrees and says, 'A woman who gives her child her last piece of bread or a soldier who dies fighting for his country are regarded as heroes. Old people who no longer wish to live and would like to see their hospital bed given to a patient with a fuller prospect of life should be similarly treated.'

As a footnote to this section on euthanasia in Holland, it is worth recording a comment on it made by the BMA report already referred to. 'The techniques developed in the Netherlands,' its authors blandly declare, 'mean that the opportunity for reflection is unlikely to be available to a person when a doctor acts to terminate their life.' This is quite untrue. As any doctor in Holland who practises euthanasia will tell you, the request for it has to be sustained over a period of time, and the patient can withdraw the request whenever he chooses.

SO WHAT changes would one like to see here?

Firstly it would be helpful if every doctor's surgery in the country could keep supplies of what the Americans call Living Wills and we in this country call Advance Declarations, and that patients be encouraged to complete and return them. Here is the form as prepared by the Voluntary Euthanasia Society and obtainable from them at their offices at 13 Prince of Wales Terrace, London W8.

TO MY FAMILY AND MY PHYSICIAN

This Declaration is made by me............................

....

at a time when I am of sound mind and after careful consideration.

If I am unable to take part in decisions about my medical care owing to my physical or mental incapacity and if I develop one or more of the medical conditions listed in Item Three below and two independent physicians conclude that there is no prospect of my recovery, I declare that my wishes are as follows:

1. I request that my life shall not be sustained by artificial means such as life support systems,

intravenous fluids or drugs, or by tube feeding.

2. I request that distressing symptoms caused either by the illness or by lack of food or fluid should be controlled by appropriate sedative treatment, even though such treatment may shorten my life.
3. The said medical conditions are:
   (1) Severe and lasting brain damage sustained as a result of injury, including stroke, or disease.
   (2) Advanced disseminated malignant disease.
   (3) Advanced degenerative disease of the nervous and/or muscular systems with severe limitations of independent mobility, and no satisfactory response to treatment.
   (4) Senile or pre-senile dementia e.g. Alzheimer or multi-infarct type.
   (5) Other condition of comparable gravity.

* Cross out and initial any condition you do not with to include.

I further declare that I hereby absolve my medical attendants from any civil liability arising from action taken in response to and in terms of this Declaration.

I reserve my right to revoke this Declaration at any time.

(Signed in the presence of two witnesses)

It is also suggested that those who sign the Declaration appoint a surrogate (a solicitor or family friend) or two (in case one dies) to ensure that if the need should ever arise the Declaration is carried out: this is best achieved by making out a deed giving the surrogate a special power of attorney.

In addition it is recommended that application be made to the Voluntary Euthanasia Society for the issue of a green Medical Emergency Card to be carried on the person. I keep mine in my wallet in case of accident. It reads as follows:

My full name is

....

Please contact

....

....

1. My blood group is...

2. Medical information

....

....

3. If there is no reasonable prospect of recovery I do NOT wish to be resuscitated or my life to be artificially prolonged.

(Tick)

4. After death my organs may be used for medical purposes.

(Tick)

Signature Date

In the majority of states in America execution of a Living Will is now mandatory, while the Advance Declaration is only advisory. There seems no reason why it should not be made mandatory too; for there can be nothing more futile or more wasteful of hospital resources and human time and effort than keeping artificially alive those who have slid into a persistent and irreversible vegetative state such as the latter stages of Alzheimer's Disease.

No Advance Declaration however is going to be of any help to that other distressing group of cases to which voluntary euthanasia cannot apply . . . I mean that of severely malformed infants. Modern medical techniques now often make it possible to spot severe malformation in the womb and then, should the mother wish it, to bring about an abortion. For those cases where a severely malformed infant is born, doctors in the past have, at the mother's request, taken steps by way of heavy sedation and dehydration to see that the infant does not survive; and they will no doubt continue to do so.

On the larger scale what is needed is a simple amendment to the 1961 Suicide Act to make it no longer a crime for a fully qualified member of the medical profession to assist a patient to die, provided similar safeguards to those laid down by the Rotterdam Court are observed. I would add another, that the doctor who performs the euthanasia declares that he expects no material benefits from the patient's death, and if it later emerges that he has been left a legacy by the patient, he shall not be permitted to receive it, unless its value be less than, say, £100.

There is another caveat I would strongly press for. Once voluntary euthanasia has been legalised, there will inevitably be media interest to find out who in Britain was the first person on whom it was legally performed, together with reactions from the doctor, next of kin, etc. To avoid this, then and on all subsequent occasions, I suggest that the only official who needs to be informed that euthanasia has taken place is the local coroner, and that an amendment be made to the Coroner's Act of 1988 to bring its proceedings, at least in this respect, into line with those of Scotland where they are conducted entirely in private and findings are never made public. Thus the privacy (for death is a very private matter) of both the doctor and the family would be protected. I imagine that in most cases the proceedings would be without dispute, but should the coroner have any cause for doubts, he has the power to send for the doctor and next of kin and, if still unsatisfied, inform the police and the Director of Public Prosecutions.

As for the manner of death, I agree with Dr Admiraal that the most desirable method is for the patient himself to take a draught prepared by the doctor and in his presence, because then the responsibility for the act is primarily the patient's, with the doctor in the passive role of adviser and assistant. Indeed in the distant future I can envisage a situation where a very old person, not necessarily terminally ill but like my mother utterly exhausted by life, might well decide that the time had come to (in her phrase) be gathered, and before arranging for it, invite his or her nearest and dearest for a farewell glass of wine or champagne. Yet many, perhaps most, of those desirous of death will be too far gone to know or care how it is done, so long as it is done swiftly, and for them there will be no objection to a lethal intravenous injection.

As of today the whole euthanasia debate can be summed up as a conflict between two very powerful and conflicting emotions: on the one hand the fear that if voluntary euthanasia is legalised, it will in time slide imperceptibly into compulsory euthanasia, and we shall all be in danger of being snuffed out before our time; and on the other the fear that if euthanasia is not legalised, we may have to face a future of degraded senility, our last days passed wired to machines, unable to control our bodily functions, all love of living gone. It seems to me that the first fear is an irrational one, being speculative and based on ignorance, but that the second fear is well-founded, being based on what we know is happening in every hospital and in many homes in the land.

Because of that I am of the opinion that whereas say 20 years ago the first fear would have had precedence in most people's minds, today it is increasingly the second. Like Drs Admiraal and Cohen and all their colleagues in Holland, like Drs Barnard and Brewer and Clark and Miller and Henderson-Smith, like Professor Fletcher in America and the members of the 31 Voluntary Euthanasia Societies scattered around the world, I believe the movement can little longer be resisted; and this pamphlet will have been well worth writing if it helps to speed it on its way.

People ask about safeguards. My correspondent who became a supporter of euthanasia after his mother had tried to cut her arteries wrote to me: 'I cannot believe it is beyond the wit of man to devise adequate safeguards.' Nor can I. I believe that those established in Holland together with those I have outlined here are sufficient to prevent abuse; and there may be others worth considering. But never in the history of mankind has any major human advance been made without some degree of risk. Columbus when he sailed to America and the astronauts when they voyaged to the moon, accepted the risks they knew they were taking, or they would not have gone. All one can do about risks, when pushing forward the frontiers of human endeavour and experience, is to see they are kept to a minimum. The alternative, of doing nothing, is in my view no longer acceptable.

When people heard I was writing this pamphlet, they asked if I did not find the subject a gloomy one. Far from it. What I do find gloomy is the thought of the needless miseries now being endured by millions because societies have lacked the courage until now to seek to bring about a change in the law. Yet it is not only the law that has to change, but our attitudes. What is needed is a totally new view of death, so that it is no longer a taboo subject, so that we are no longer afraid of it – of dying, yes, that is what this pamphlet has been about – but not of death itself (though paradoxically this will be easier for those who have come to accept the idea of their own mortality).

It is time we listened to the poets, Shelley's 'unacknowledged legislators', who for centuries have been urging us to treat death not as an enemy but as a friend.

> If I must die,
> I will encounter darkness as a bride,
> And hug it in my arms

Yes. And for those for whom the light is already draining from the sky, let it be sooner rather than later.

About the Author

LUDOVIC KENNEDY is a distinguished writer and broadcaster. On television he has presented *The World at One*, *Face the Press*, *Midweek* and *Did You See?* His books include *Ten Rillington Place*, *The Trial of Stephen Ward*, *The Portland Spy Case* and *The Airman and the Carpenter*. His autobiography, *On My Way to the Club*, was published in 1989.

CHATTO

CounterBlasts

Also available in bookshops now:-

No. 1	Jonathan Raban	**God, Man & Mrs Thatcher**
No. 2	Paul Foot	**Ireland:** Why Britain Must Get Out
No. 3	John Lloyd	**A Rational Advance for the Labour Party**
No. 4	Fay Weldon	**Sacred Cows:** A Portrait of Britain, post-Rushdie, pre-Utopia
No. 5	Marina Warner	**Into the Dangerous World**
No. 6	William Shawcross	**Kowtow!**
No. 7	Ruth Rendell and Colin Ward	**Undermining the Central Line**
No. 8	Mary Warnock	**Universities:** Knowing Our Minds
No. 9	Sue Townsend	**Mr Bevan's Dream**
No. 10	Christopher Hitchens	**The Monarchy**
No. 11	Tessa Blackstone	**Prisons and Penal Reform**
No. 12	Douglas Dunn	**Poll Tax: The Fiscal Fake**

Forthcoming Chatto Counter*Blasts*

No. 14	Adam Mars-Jones	**Venus Envy**
No. 15	Adam Lively	**Parliament:** The Great British Democracy Swindle
No. 16	Peter Fuller	**Left High and Dry**
No. 17	Margaret Drabble	**Safe as Houses**
No. 18	Ronald Dworkin	**A Bill of Rights for Britain**

Plus pamphlets from Michael Holroyd, Hanif Kureishi, Michael Ignatieff and Susannah Clapp

If you want to join in the debate, and if you want to know more about **Counter*Blasts***, the writers and the issues, then write to:

Random Century Group, Freepost 5066, Dept MH, London SW1V 2YY